ZOO ANIMALS
IN THE WILD

TIGER

JINNY JOHNSON
ILLUSTRATED BY MICHAEL WOODS

FRANKLIN WATTS
LONDON•SYDNEY

An Appleseed Editions book

First published in 2005 by Franklin Watts
96 Leonard Street, London EC2A 4XD

Franklin Watts Australia
Level 17/207 Kent Street, Sydney, NSW 2000

Created by Appleseed Editions Ltd,
Well House, Friars Hill, Guestling, East Sussex TN35 4ET

Designed by Helen James
Illustrated by Michael Woods

ISBN 0 7496 5976 9

A CIP catalogue for this book is available from the British Library

Photographs by Corbis (Bettmann, Tom Brakefield, W. Perry Conway, Tim Davis, Gallo Images, W. Wayne
Lockwood, M.D., Renee Lynn, YURIKO NAKAO/Reuters, Phillip Perry; Frank Lane Picture Agency, Reuters,
Kennan Ward), Photri (Dinodia), Wildlife Conservation Society (D. Shapiro)

Printed and bound in Thailand

Contents

Tigers 4

Stripy tigers 6

At home in the wild 8

At home in the zoo 10

Tigers in action 12

New arrivals 14

Family life 16

A tiger's day 18

Feeding time 20

Time for play 22

Learning to hunt 24

Growing up 26

Tiger fact file 28

Words to remember 30

Index 32

Tigers

Tigers are the biggest of all the big cats. A male tiger weighs more than three or four full-grown men and female tigers are only slightly smaller. Tigers are very powerful hunters. They live by catching other animals to eat.

A tiger has big teeth and sharp claws. The claws can be pulled back into special covers called sheaths. This stops them from getting blunt as the tiger moves. A tiger's paws are just like those of a pet cat – but much bigger! The paws have thick pads underneath, so the tiger can walk around very quietly.

There aren't very many tigers left in the wild, so it is important that there are some living happily in zoos. The tigers you see at the zoo have all been born in zoos or wildlife parks. They have not been taken from the wild.

A tiger has 30 teeth. The biggest can be up to 7.5 cm long.

A tiger's paw print is called a pug mark. No two tigers have exactly the same pug mark.

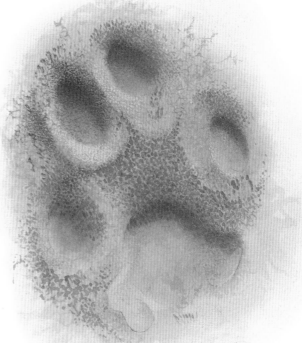

5

Stripy tigers

All tigers have stripy fur. Most of the fur is golden-brown with dark stripes, but a tiger's tummy is a lighter colour.

A tiger's stripy coat helps it stay hidden when it goes hunting. The stripes make it harder for other animals to see the shape of the tiger's body. The tiger creeps up on the animal it is hunting (its prey) and gets as close as possible before it pounces.

A tiger's stripes make it hard to see as it stands in the long grass.

Some zoos have tigers with white fur and tan stripes. These white tigers have blue eyes. Most other tigers have yellow eyes.

No two tigers have exactly the same pattern of stripes. They are all slightly different – just as people all have different fingerprints.

At home in the wild

Wild tigers live in forests, woods and grasslands. They like to be where there are plenty of plants to hide among as they watch for prey. Tigers need to be near fresh water too, so they have plenty to drink.

Not all tigers live in hot countries. Some tigers live in a very cold part of the world called Siberia. There's a lot of snow there in the winter, so the tigers need extra-thick fur to keep them warm.

Every tiger has its own home range, where it lives and finds all its food.

This area is called a territory. A tiger marks its territory by scratching trees or scraping the ground with its back feet. It also leaves droppings to tell other tigers to stay away.

This tiger is making a mark to other tigers to say, 'Keep out. This area is mine.' Scratching helps to keep a tiger's claws sharp, too.

Tigers roar as a signal to other tigers to say, 'I'm here. Watch out.'

Tigers usually live alone – except for mother tigers raising cubs.

At home in the zoo

More than 1,200 tigers live in zoos all over the world. Most zoos want their animals to be happy and comfortable. So they try to make the tiger's home in the zoo like the wild places where it lives.

A tiger's home in a zoo needs plenty of trees and plants and some rocks or logs to lie on. There should also be somewhere for the tiger to hide when it doesn't feel like being stared at.

Some zoos keep the rocks in a tiger's enclosure cool in summer and warm in winter.

In the wild, tigers check their home area for the smells of other tigers. In the zoo, keepers spread different scents, such as the smells of other animals and even spicy smells such as cinnamon, to keep the tigers interested.

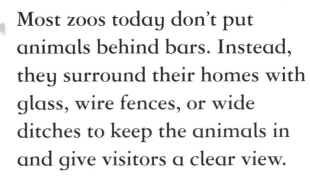

Most zoos today don't put animals behind bars. Instead, they surround their homes with glass, wire fences, or wide ditches to keep the animals in and give visitors a clear view.

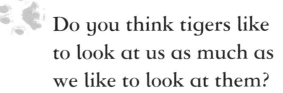

Do you think tigers like to look at us as much as we like to look at them?

Tigers in action

Tigers can run fast but only for very short distances. They are good jumpers and can make giant leaps of more than ten metres as they pounce on their prey.

A tiger's powerful leg muscles help it make big jumps.

A tiger can run at 55 kilometres an hour for a few minutes. That's much faster than the fastest human.

Most cats, big and small, don't like to get wet, but tigers do. A tiger is happy to splash into water and can swim well. On a hot day, a tiger likes nothing better than a refreshing dip in a river.

Zoos try to make sure there is a pool in a tiger's home. where it can swim and splash when it wants.

New arrivals

A mother tiger gives birth to her cubs in a cosy den. Her den may be in a cave or among rocks or thick plants – anywhere she can keep her cubs well hidden from danger. She usually has two or three cubs, but she can have as many as six!

The baby tigers are blind, helpless little creatures when they are first born. Each one weighs only about as much as a bag of sugar (1–1.5 kg). They stay close to their mother, who keeps them safe. She cleans them by licking their bodies with her rough tongue.

A cub's eyes start to open when it is about a week old.

A mother tiger takes care of her cubs by herself. Male tigers live on their own and are not part of the family.

A mother tiger in a zoo is usually moved to a separate enclosure away from other tigers before her cubs are born. She stays there until her cubs are at least two or three months old.

Family life

Tiger cubs drink only their mother's milk for the first six to eight weeks of their lives. This milk contains everything they need to help them grow.

When her cubs are a couple of months old, their mother starts bringing them meat to eat. The cubs must stay hidden in their den while their mother is away hunting. If they peek out, they might be caught and eaten by other hunters such as eagles or wild dogs called jackals.

As the cubs grow bigger, the keepers in the zoo start to feed them a bit of meat. But the young tigers still like to have their milk too!

Mum is out hunting and these cubs are hoping she will bring back a tasty supper.

If a mother tiger thinks her cubs might be in danger, she moves them to another den. She picks up each cub in her mouth and carries it carefully to its new home.

A tiger's day

Tigers love to sleep. They spend most of the day sprawled comfortably under a shady tree. But tigers aren't lazy. They are saving their strength for the hard work of hunting.

Towards the end of the afternoon, a tiger family begins to wake up. Cubs start to play and chase each other. Their mother often cleans her fur before going off to hunt.

A tiger spends time cleaning its fur every day.

Like tigers in the wild, tigers in the zoo may spend as much as 18 hours a day just lying around.

A tiger cleans itself with its tongue. The tongue is very rough because it is covered with tiny hooks. These hooks help to scrape dirt off the fur. They also help to scrape meat off bones when the tiger eats.

A mother tiger licks her cubs to keep them clean.

19

Feeding time

Tigers usually go hunting late in the evening or at night. They see well in the dark, and their ears pick up the slightest sound. A tiger may have to walk a long way before it spots a prey animal – perhaps a deer or a wild pig.

The tiger crouches down and watches the animal before moving forward a little at a time. When the tiger is as close as it can get to its prey, it rushes out and attacks. But about nine times out of ten the tiger doesn't catch its prey.

A mother tiger takes her catch back to her cubs. They eat as much as they can, then rest for a while before eating some more.

A full-grown tiger can gulp down as much as 18 kg of meat in one meal. That's like eating about 80 large steaks!

Animals such as deer can run very fast – faster than tigers – and often escape. Sometimes, if a tiger can't catch a large animal, it will hunt for smaller ones such as birds and lizards.

Tigers in the zoo are given about 5–6 kg of meat a day, as well as some bones. Chewing bones helps to keep the tigers' teeth sharp.

Time for play

Tiger cubs love to play. They chase one another, pounce and wrestle. They run after butterflies and try to catch them. If they dare, they even pounce on their mother's tail as it flicks back and forth.

Tiger cubs don't usually hurt each other when they play fight. It's just a good way to practise for when they are grown-up hunters.

Zookeepers give tigers toys to play with. These toys may include balls, tyres or animal skins which the tiger can drag around.

The cubs' games are more important than they look. As they play, the cubs are practising the skills they will need later when they start hunting. Playing helps to make them stronger too. When they are a little older, the cubs will practise chasing and catching small animals such as mice and lizards.

Learning to hunt

When tiger cubs are about six months old, their mother starts to take them hunting. The cubs have a lot to learn.

At first, the cubs follow their mother and watch her carefully. They must stay very still and quiet while she sneaks up on her prey. Later, they start to help her hunt, or catch small animals by themselves.

A full-grown tiger doesn't need to hunt every night. It may catch one large animal a week and feed on it for several days. Before leaving a catch, a tiger covers it with leaves and grass to hide it from other creatures. A mother with a young family may need to hunt more often to keep her hungry cubs well fed.

As this tiger slowly creeps up on her prey, her cubs stay hidden nearby and watch her every move.

Tigers cover their catch with leaves and grasses to keep it safe for the next day.

Growing up

From 6 to 18 months of age, cubs learn how to survive by themselves. Their mother teaches them how to find and catch food and where to find water.

A young female tiger is ready to start her own family when she is three or four years old.

By the time the cubs are about 18 months old, they are nearly as big as their mother. She has taught the young tigers all she knows, and they are strong enough to hunt for their own food. The cubs will soon leave their mother to find their own home ranges.

When a cub in a zoo is old enough to leave its mother, it may be taken to another zoo to live. A tiger in a zoo usually lives longer than a tiger in the wild. Zoo tigers can live for 16-20 years.

Tiger fact file

Here is some more information about tigers.
Your mum or dad might like to read this,
or you could read these pages together.

A tiger is a mammal and belongs to the cat family.
All cats are carnivores, which means they eat meat.

Where tigers live

There are several different subspecies (or kinds) of tigers, which differ
slightly in size and colour. Siberian tigers are the biggest tigers; they
have the palest fur, and live furthest north. Tigers living further south,
such as the Sumatran tiger, are smaller and have darker-coloured fur.

Bengal tiger: Bangladesh, Bhutan, Burma, India, Nepal
Chinese tiger: China
Indochinese tiger: Burma, Vietnam, Malay Peninsula, Thailand
Siberian tiger: Russia, China, Korea
Sumatran tiger: Sumatra

There were once three other subspecies – the Caspian, Javan
and Bali tigers – but they are all now extinct.

Tiger numbers

Tigers are becoming rare and have disappeared from some areas. There are only about 5,000 to 7,500 tigers left in the world. Most are in India. The World Wildlife Fund (WWF) has set up safe areas, or reserves, there. But even there hunters kill them for their fur and parts of their bodies used in traditional Chinese medicine.

Size

A tiger measures 1.4–2.8 metres long, with a tail about 0.6–1.1 metres long. A male tiger weighs 100–305 kg; a female weighs 65–170 kg.

Find out more

Check out these websites.
5 Tigers:
The Tiger Information Center
www.5tigers.org

Wildlife Conservation Society:
Saving Tigers www.savingtigers.com

World Wildlife Fund: Tigers
www.worldwildlife.org/tigers/index.cfm

San Diego Zoo: Tigers
www.sandiegozoo.org/animalbytes/
t-tiger.html

Words to remember

cub
A young animal.

enclosure
The area where an animal lives
in a zoo.

extinct
An animals is extinct when there
are no more of that kind left alive.

jackal
An animal that looks like a small
wolf. Some attack tiger cubs or steal
the leftovers from a tiger's meal.

Mammal
A warm-blooded animal, usually with four legs
and some hair on its body. Female mammals feed
their babies with milk from their own bodies.

prey
An animal that is hunted and eaten
by another animal.

territory
The area where an animal spends
most of its time and finds its food.

Index

cubs 14, 15, 16, 18, 22, 23,
   24–25, 26, 27, 30

den 14, 16

fur 6, 7, 8, 18, 19

hunting 4, 6, 16, 18, 20–21,
   23, 24, 25, 27

prey 8, 20–21, 25, 31

running 12

size 4, 14, 29
sleeping 18
subspecies 28
swimming 13

territory 8–9, 31
threats 16
tiger numbers 29
tongue 14, 19